W6-AJH-946

.15

D0536834

Walla W...
County Libraries

COOL BACKYARD GRILLING

Beyond the Basics for Kids Who Cook

LISA
WAGNER

A Division of ABDO

ABDO
Publishing Company

Visit us at www.abdopublishing.com

Published by ABDO Publishing Company, P.O. Box 398166, Minneapolis, MN 55439. Copyright ©2014 by Abdo Consulting Group, Inc. International copyrights reserved in all countries. No part of this book may be reproduced in any form without written permission from the publisher. The Checkerboard Library™ is a trademark and logo of ABDO Publishing Company.

Printed in the United States of America,
North Mankato, Minnesota
102013
012014

 PRINTED ON RECYCLED PAPER

Editor: Liz Salzmann
Content Developer: Nancy Tuminelly
Cover and Interior Design and Production:
Colleen Dolphin, Mighty Media, Inc.
Food Production: Desirée Bussiere
Photo Credits: Colleen Dolphin, Shutterstock

Library of Congress Cataloging-in-Publication Data
Wagner, Lisa, 1958- author.
  Cool backyard grilling : beyond the basics for kids who cook / Lisa Wagner.
       pages cm. -- (Cool young chefs)
  Audience: Ages 8 to 12.
  Includes index.
  ISBN 978-1-62403-085-7
  1. Barbecuing--Juvenile literature. 2. Outdoor cooking--Juvenile literature. I. Title.
  TX840.B3W317 2014
  641.5'784--dc23
                    2013022523

TO ADULT HELPERS

Congratulations on being the proud parent of an up-and-coming chef! This series of books is designed for children who have already done some cooking—most likely with your guidance and encouragement. Now, with some of the basics out of the way, it's time to really get cooking!

The focus of this series is on parties and special events. The "Big Idea" is all about the creative side of cooking (mastering a basic method or recipe and then using substitutions to create original recipes). Listening to your young chef's ideas for new creations and sharing your own ideas and experiences can lead to exciting (and delicious) discoveries!

While the recipes are designed to let children cook independently as much as possible, you'll need to set some ground rules for using the kitchen, tools, and ingredients. Most importantly, adult supervision is a must whenever a child uses the stove, oven, or sharp tools. Look for these symbols:

Your assistance, patience, and praise will pay off with tasty rewards for the family, and invaluable life skills for your child. Let the adventures in cooking beyond the basics begin!

CONTENTS

GRILL UP A GREAT PARTY!

Welcome to Cool Young Chefs! If you have already used other Cool Cooking books, this series is for you. You know how to read a recipe and how to prepare ingredients. You have learned about measuring, cooking tools, and kitchen safety. Best of all, you like to cook!

This book is all about grilling great foods. You can grill on a gas, electric, or charcoal grill. You'll get a different flavor on each one. The recipes in this book were made specially for a gas grill, but with practice you can get a great flavor from any grill.

USE CAUTION!

All surfaces of a grill can be hot, inside and out. Use oven mitts, long-handled cooking tools, and caution. Have an adult light the grill and stay nearby when it is in use.

DON'T FORGET DESSERT!

Here are some easy favorites.

- watermelon
- fresh fruit salad
- ice cream cones or sundaes
- fruit **cobbler**
- berry shortcakes

MAKE IT A PARTY!

At a grilling party, the grilled food will be the star of the show. Simple side dishes can be prepared ahead of time. Here are some popular sides for grilled foods.

- coleslaw
- potato salad
- bean salad
- **marinated** vegetable salad
- mixed green salad
- chips

5

WHAT'S THE BIG IDEA?

Besides being a good cook, a chef is prepared, **efficient**, organized, resourceful, creative, and adventurous. The Big Idea in *Cool Backyard Grilling* is all about being adventurous.

Learning new recipes and **techniques** is always an adventure! In this book you get to take your cooking adventure outside.

You will learn about making **marinades** and rubs to flavor grilled food. Marinades are liquid mixtures of herbs, spices, oils, and **condiments**. Rubs are dry mixtures of herbs and spices. Both marinades and rubs can contain sugar or honey to help **caramelize** grilled food.

Always use grill tongs to turn food and remove it from the grill. Using a fork will poke holes in the surface and juices will be lost. The juices help keep the food moist and tender.

FIRST THINGS FIRST

A successful chef is smart, careful, and patient. Take time to review the basics before you start cooking. After that, get creative and have some fun!

BE SMART, BE SAFE

- Start with clean hands, tools, and work surfaces.
- Always get **permission** to use the kitchen, cooking tools, and ingredients.
- Ask an adult when you need help or have questions.
- Always have an adult nearby when you use the stove, oven, grill, or sharp tools.
- Prevent accidents by working slowly and carefully.

NO GERMS ALLOWED

After you handle raw eggs or raw meat, wash your hands with soap and water. Wash tools and work surfaces with soap and water too. Raw eggs and raw meat have bacteria that don't survive when the food is cooked. But the bacteria can survive at room or body temperature. These bacteria can make you very sick if you consume them. So, keep everything clean!

BE PREPARED

- Read through the entire recipe before you do anything else!
- Gather all the tools and ingredients you will need.
- Wash fruits and vegetables well. Pat them dry with a **towel**.
- Get the ingredients ready. The list of ingredients tells how to prepare each item.
- If you see a word you don't know, check the **glossary** on page 30.
- Do the steps in the order they are listed.

GOOD COOKING TAKES TIME

- Allow plenty of time to prepare your recipes.
- Be patient with yourself. **Prep** work can take a long time at first.

ONE LAST THING

- When you are done cooking, wash all the dishes and **utensils**.
- Clean up your work area and put away any unused ingredients.

KEY SYMBOLS

In this book, you will see some symbols beside the recipes. Here is what they mean.

The recipe requires the use of a grill, stove, or oven. You need adult **supervision** and assistance.

A sharp tool such as a peeler, knife, or **grater** is needed. Be extra careful, and get an adult to stand by.

BEYOND COOL

Remember the Big Idea? In the Beyond Cool boxes, you will find ideas to help you create your own recipes. Once you learn a recipe, you will be able to make many **versions** of it. Remember, being able to make original recipes turns cooks into chefs!

When you modify a recipe, be sure to write down what you did. If anyone asks for your recipe, you will be able to share it proudly.

GET THE PICTURE

When a step number in a recipe has a circle around it with an arrow, it will point to the picture that shows how to do the step.

③ →

COOL TIP

These tips can help you do something faster, better, or more easily.

UNIQUELY COOL

Here are some of the **techniques**, tools, and ingredients used in this book.

TECHNIQUE:

SEED A CUCUMBER

Use a vegetable peeler to remove the peel. Trim off the ends and cut the cucumber in half the long way. Scrape the seeds out with a spoon.

TOOLS:

CHARCOAL GRILL

GAS GRILL

ZESTER

GRATER

GRILL GRATE

GRILL TONGS

GRILL SPATULA

STRAINER

JUICER

INGREDIENTS:

CAPERS

FETA CHEESE

ZUCCHINI
SQUASH

FRESH
PARSLEY

FRESH DILL

SCALLIONS

FRESH TUNA

CILANTRO

GREEK
YOGURT

YELLOW
SQUASH

BREAD CRUMBS

DIJON
MUSTARD

TASTY BASIC BURGER

ingredients

1 pound ground beef

1 egg

⅓ cup dry bread crumbs

½ teaspoon pepper

2 teaspoons Worcestershire sauce

vegetable oil

salt

4 hamburger buns

tools

measuring spoons

measuring cups

large mixing bowl

grill tongs

paper towels

grill spatula

1. Have an adult preheat the grill to medium-high heat.

2. Put the ground beef, egg, bread crumbs, pepper, and Worcestershire sauce in a mixing bowl. Mix with your hands until well blended.

3. Divide the mixture into fourths. Shape each piece into a ¾-inch-thick **patty**. Make a small dent in the center to keep the patty from swelling.

4. Lightly oil the **grate**. Place the patties on the grill. Sprinkle them with salt. Cook the **patties** for 5 to 7 minutes on each side. Serve them on buns with all your favorite toppings.

COOL TIP

To oil the grate, first fold a paper **towel** into a small pad. Hold the paper towel pad with grill tongs. Dip it in a bowl of vegetable oil and wipe it over the grate.

BEYOND COOL

- You can add other seasonings to the meat. Make combinations from this list, or invent your own.
  - > lemon pepper or other seasoned pepper
  - > fresh or dried herbs such as oregano, parsley, basil, thyme, or dill
  - > onion powder or garlic powder
  - > **minced** fresh garlic or minced fresh onion
- Ketchup and mustard are the most popular **condiments** served with burgers. Be adventurous and try something different! Some ideas include barbecue sauce, teriyaki sauce, hot pepper sauce, blue cheese **dressing**, and pizza sauce.
- After you flip the burgers, top each with a slice of cheese. Use any kind of cheese you like.

13

GYRO BURGER WITH TZATZIKI

ingredients

TZATZIKI

1 cucumber, peeled, seeded, and grated using the largest holes on the grater

1 16-ounce container of Greek yogurt

juice from 1 lemon

3 cloves garlic, minced

½ teaspoon salt

BURGERS

1 pound ground beef

1 egg

1 small onion, minced

2 cloves garlic, minced

¼ cup dry bread crumbs

¼ teaspoon allspice

½ teaspoon cinnamon

½ teaspoon cumin

1 teaspoon dried dill weed

½ teaspoon black pepper

vegetable oil

salt

4 hamburger buns

tools

vegetable peeler

spoon

grater

sharp knife

cutting board

measuring cups & spoons

mixing bowls

mixing spoon

grill tongs

paper towels

grill spatula

1. Put all of the **tzatziki** ingredients in a small mixing bowl. Mix well. Chill for at least 1 hour before serving.

2. Have an adult preheat the grill to medium-high heat.

3. Put the ground beef, egg, onion, garlic, bread crumbs, allspice, cinnamon, cumin, dill weed, and pepper in a mixing bowl. Mix with your hands until well blended.

4. Divide the mixture into fourths. Shape each piece into a ¾-inch-thick **patty**. Make a small dent in the center to keep the patty from swelling.

5. Lightly oil the **grate** (See Cool Tip on page 13).

6. Place the patties on the grill. Sprinkle them with salt. Cook the patties for 5 to 7 minutes on each side. Serve them on buns with tzatziki.

BEYOND COOL

- Add ¼ cup of chopped fresh cilantro to the burgers.
- Use 1 tablespoon fresh dill instead of the dried dill.
- Add 1 cup of **crumbled** feta cheese to the meat mixture.

15

SPICY BLACK BEAN BURGER

ingredients

vegetable oil

1 16-ounce can black beans, drained and rinsed

½ red pepper, minced

½ red onion, minced

2 cloves garlic, minced

1 egg

1 teaspoon cumin

1 teaspoon hot pepper sauce

1 tablespoon chile powder

about ½ cup dry bread crumbs

4 hamburger buns

tools

heavy-duty aluminum foil

can opener

strainer

sharp knife

cutting board

measuring spoons

measuring cups

large mixing bowl

fork

mixing spoon

small mixing bowl

whisk

grill tongs

paper towels

grill spatula

1. Have an adult preheat the grill to high heat. Coat a sheet of heavy-duty aluminum foil with vegetable oil. Set the foil aside.

2. Put the beans in a large mixing bowl. Use a fork to mash the beans to a paste.

3. Add the red pepper, onion, and garlic. Mix well.

4. Whisk the egg with cumin, hot pepper sauce, and chile powder together in a small mixing bowl. Add the egg mixture to the bean mixture. Stir until everything is well blended.

5. Add the bread crumbs. Mix with your hands. The mixture should be sticky and hold together when pressed. Add more bread crumbs if the mixture doesn't hold together.

6. Divide the mixture into fourths. Shape each piece into a ¾-inch-thick **patty**.

7. Place the patties on the greased foil. Place the foil on the grill. Cook over high heat for about 7 minutes on each side. Serve them on buns with your favorite toppings.

WORLD'S BEST TUNA BURGER

ingredients

1 pound fresh tuna, cut into ¾-inch cubes

½ small red onion, minced

2 tablespoons capers, rinsed, drained, and chopped

¼ cup chopped fresh parsley

1 tablespoon olive oil

1 tablespoon Dijon mustard

2 teaspoons lemon juice

1 teaspoon Worcestershire sauce

½ teaspoon salt

¼ teaspoon black pepper

about 1 cup dry bread crumbs

vegetable oil

6 hamburger buns

lettuce leaves

thin slices of red onion

tools

sharp knife

cutting board

strainer

measuring spoons

measuring cups

large mixing bowl

mixing spoon

grill tongs

paper towels

grill spatula

1 Have an adult preheat the grill to medium-high heat.

2 Put the tuna, onion, capers, parsley, olive oil, Dijon mustard, lemon juice, Worcestershire sauce, salt, and pepper in a mixing bowl. Mix gently until the ingredients are combined.

3 Mix in enough bread crumbs so the mixture holds together when pressed.

4 Divide the mixture into sixths. Shape each piece into a ¾-inch-thick **patty**.

5 Lightly oil the **grate** (See Cool Tip on page 13)

6 Place the patties on the grill. Cook the patties for 4 to 5 minutes on each side. Serve them on buns with Dijon mustard, lettuce, and sliced red onion.

BEYOND COOL

- For a crunchier coating, use 1 cup Panko bread crumbs and 1 cup dried bread crumbs. Panko bread crumbs are **available** in the Asian sections of many **grocery stores**.

- Substitute 2 tablespoons chopped fresh dill for the parsley.

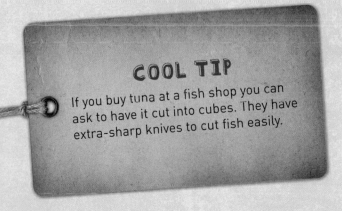

COOL TIP

If you buy tuna at a fish shop you can ask to have it cut into cubes. They have extra-sharp knives to cut fish easily.

CHICKEN WINGS WITH SPICE RUB

ingredients

3 pounds chicken wings
1 tablespoon lemon pepper
1 tablespoon garlic powder
1 tablespoon onion powder
1 tablespoon dry mustard
1 tablespoon chile powder
1 tablespoon black pepper
1 tablespoon salt
1 tablespoon cumin
1 tablespoon brown sugar
3 tablespoons paprika
vegetable oil

tools

paper towels
baking sheet
measuring spoons
whisk
large mixing bowl
mixing spoon
plastic wrap
grill tongs
paper towels

CHILL BEFORE YOU GRILL!

Allow at least 3 hours to make these wings. They need time to chill before you grill.

20

1. Wash the chicken wings and pat them dry with paper **towels**. Place them on a baking sheet and refrigerate for at least 1 hour.

2. Whisk all of the dry ingredients together in a large mixing bowl.

3. Put the chilled chicken wings in the bowl. Toss to coat the wings with the spices. **Discard** any leftover spices. Cover the bowl with plastic wrap. Return to the refrigerator for 1 more hour.

4. Have an adult preheat the grill to medium heat. Lightly oil the **grate** (See Cool Tip on page 13).

5. Place the chicken wings on the grill. Cook 5 minutes on each side with the grill open. Cover the grill and continue cooking until the wings are cooked through. Total cooking time will be from 20 to 40 minutes, depending on the size of the wings.

BEYOND COOL

Invent your own spice rub! Just make sure not to use too much salt. Try adding ingredients such as celery salt or garlic salt (replace or cut back on other salt used), cayenne pepper, dried thyme, dried oregano, dried basil, ground bay leaves, and ground coriander seed.

MARINATED CHICKEN KEBABS

ingredients

1 pound boneless, skinless chicken breasts

1 8-ounce container Greek yogurt

zest of 1 lemon

juice from 1 lemon

2 teaspoons dried oregano

½ teaspoon salt

¼ teaspoon black pepper

1 large red onion, cut into wedges

1 green bell pepper, cut into 1-inch pieces

1 yellow squash, cut into ½-inch slices

vegetable oil

tools

zester or grater

measuring spoons

sharp knife

cutting board

paper towels

9 × 9-inch baking dish

mixing spoon

plastic wrap

bamboo skewers

grill tongs

MARINATE!

Allow plenty of time. The chicken needs to **marinate** for 2 to 3 hours before grilling.

1. Wash the chicken and pat it dry with paper **towels**. Cut the chicken into 1-inch cubes.

2. Whisk the yogurt, lemon **zest**, lemon juice, oregano, salt, and pepper together in the baking dish.

3. Put the chicken in the dish. Mix to coat the chicken with **marinade**. Cover the dish with plastic wrap and marinate for 2 to 3 hours in the refrigerator.

4. Remove the chicken pieces from the marinade. Put the pieces of chicken, onion, green pepper, and squash on the skewers. **Discard** the used marinade.

5. Have an adult preheat the grill to medium heat.

6. Lightly oil the **grate** (See Cool Tip on page 13).

7. Place the chicken kebabs on the grill. Cook for 5 minutes on each side. Continue cooking until the chicken is cooked through. Test by cutting into a piece of chicken with a sharp knife. When the meat is no longer pink and the juice is clear, the chicken is done.

BEYOND COOL

- Add other vegetables to the kebabs.
  - > mushrooms
  - > zucchini slices
  - > cherry tomatoes
- Serve with **tzatziki** (see page 15).

TERIYAKI STEAK KEBABS

ingredients

½ cup soy sauce

2 tablespoons olive oil

2 tablespoons brown sugar

3 cloves garlic, minced

¼ teaspoon black pepper

1½ pounds boneless sirloin steak, cut into 1¼-inch cubes

1 green bell pepper, cut into 1-inch pieces

12 cherry tomatoes

12 scallions, cut into 2-inch pieces

12 whole mushrooms

vegetable oil

tools

measuring cups

measuring spoons

sharp knife

cutting board

whisk

large mixing bowl

small mixing bowl

plastic wrap

mixing spoon

9 × 9-inch baking dish

bamboo skewers

basting brush

grill tongs

paper towels

MARINATE!

Allow plenty of time. The steak needs to **marinate** for at least 3 hours before grilling.

BEYOND COOL

Add 1 teaspoon of ground ginger to the marinade.

1. Whisk soy sauce, olive oil, brown sugar, garlic, and pepper together in a large mixing bowl. Put half of this **marinade** in a small bowl and cover with plastic wrap.

2. Put the steak in the large bowl. Mix to coat the meat with marinade.

3. Put the meat and marinade mixture in the baking dish. Cover with plastic wrap. Place the baking dish and the small bowl of marinade in the refrigerator. Chill for at least 3 hours and as long as overnight.

4. Remove the steak from the marinade. **Discard** the marinade. Put the meat, green pepper, scallions, and mushrooms on the skewers.

5. Have an adult preheat the grill to medium-high heat.

6. Lightly oil the **grate** (See Cool Tip on page 13).

7. Place the kebabs on the grill. Cook for 3 minutes on each side. **Baste** with marinade from the small bowl. Turn the heat down to medium. Continue grilling and turning the kebabs until the meat is cooked the way you like it. This will take between 5 and 10 minutes. Baste once more before serving.

MARINATED VEGGIE KEBABS

ingredients

½ cup olive oil

½ cup fresh lemon juice

3 cloves garlic, minced

salt and pepper

2 zucchini, cut into ½-inch slices

1 yellow squash, cut into ½-inch slices

1 green or red bell pepper, cut into 1-inch pieces

12 cherry tomatoes

1 red or white onion, cut into wedges

vegetable oil

tools

measuring cups

sharp knife

cutting board

mixing bowl

whisk

bamboo skewers

9 × 13-inch baking dish

plastic wrap

grill tongs

paper towels

MARINATE!

Allow plenty of time. The kebabs need to **marinate** for 30 to 60 minutes before grilling.

26

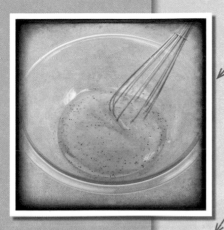

1. Whisk the olive oil, lemon juice, and garlic together in a mixing bowl until well blended. If the mixture is too sour, add more olive oil and whisk to blend. Add salt and pepper to taste.

2. Put the vegetables on the skewers.

3. Place the kebabs in the baking dish. Pour the **marinade** over the kebabs. Turn the kebabs to coat the vegetables. Cover the dish with plastic wrap and let sit for 30 to 60 minutes.

4. Have an adult preheat the grill to medium heat.

5. Lightly oil the **grate** (See Cool Tip on page 13).

6. Place the kebabs on the grill. Cook for 8 to 10 minutes. Turn them often to prevent burning. Cook until the vegetables are tender but not mushy.

BEYOND COOL

Add fresh or dried herbs to the marinade. Use up to 4 teaspoons of dried herbs in any combination. Or, use 4 tablespoons of fresh herbs, such as basil, dill, parsley, thyme, marjoram, and rosemary.

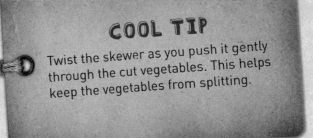

COOL TIP

Twist the skewer as you push it gently through the cut vegetables. This helps keep the vegetables from splitting.

GRILLED CORN WITH BUTTER

ingredients

8 ears fresh corn,
  husks and strings removed

vegetable oil

CHILI LIME BUTTER

½ cup unsalted butter,
  at room temperature

2 tablespoons fresh
  lime juice

1 tablespoon chile powder

1 teaspoon ground cumin

1 teaspoon black pepper

LEMON HERB BUTTER

½ cup unsalted butter,
  at room temperature

2 tablespoons fresh
  lemon juice

1 teaspoon dried basil

1 teaspoon dried oregano

1 teaspoon garlic salt

tools

measuring spoons

small bowl

fork

grill tongs

paper towels

CHILI LIME BUTTER

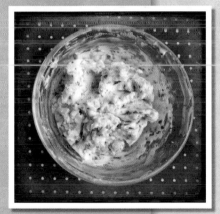

LEMON HERB BUTTER

1 Choose a flavored butter recipe to make. Put the butter ingredients in a small bowl. Beat with a fork until well blended.

2 Spread half the flavored butter on the ears of corn. Set the other half aside until serving time.

3 Have an adult preheat the grill to medium heat.

4 Lightly oil the **grate** (See Cool Tip on page 13).

5 Place the corn on the grill and cook for 6 to 8 minutes. Turn the corn often so it cooks evenly and does not burn.

6 Serve hot with the remaining flavored butter.

COOL TIP

Pick the tastiest type of corn! Look for bright green corn husks. Peel back the husk. Check the kernels. They should be plump and see-through.

BEYOND COOL

- Replace any of the dried herbs with fresh herbs. Substitute 1 tablespoon of fresh herbs for 1 teaspoon of dried herbs.

- A flavored butter is **delicious** on grilled steak or chicken too.

GLOSSARY

available – able to be had or used.

baste – to brush with liquid, such as melted fat or juices, while cooking.

caramelize – to cook sugar, syrup, or honey until it turns into caramel, a sweet, brown flavoring.

cobbler – a deep-dish fruit pie with a top crust.

condiment – something that adds flavor to food, such as a sauce or a spice.

crumble – to break into small pieces.

delicious – very pleasing to taste or smell.

discard – to throw away.

dressing – a sauce that is used in salads.

efficient – able to do something without wasting time, money, or energy.

glossary – a list of the hard or unusual words found in a book.

grate – 1. to cut something into small pieces using a grater. A grater is a tool with sharp-edged holes. 2. a frame of metal bars that forms the cooking surface of a grill.

grocery store – a store that sells mostly food items.

marinade – a sauce that food is soaked in before cooking. To marinate something means to soak it in a marinade.

mince – to cut or chop into very small pieces.

patty – a round, flat cake made with chopped food.

permission – when a person in charge says it's okay to do something.

prep – short for preparation, the work done before starting to make a recipe, such as washing fruits and vegetables, measuring, cutting, peeling, and grating.

supervision – the act of watching over or directing others.

technique – a method or style in which something is done.

towel – a cloth or paper used for cleaning or drying.

tzatziki – a traditional Greek yogurt sauce.

utensil – a tool used to prepare or eat food.

version – a different form or type from the original.

zest – small pieces of the peel of a citrus fruit, made by rubbing the fruit with a zester or grater.

WEB SITES

To learn more about cool cooking, visit ABDO Publishing Company online at www.abdopublishing.com. Web sites about cool cooking are featured on our Book Links page. These links are monitored and updated to provide the most current information available.

INDEX